SHEET PAN RECIPES

*The Ultimate and Easy to Follow Guide to
Make Perfect Meals by Using Sheet Pan in
Under 30 Minutes – A Gift for Beginners*

Table of Contents

INTRODUCTION

At the point when you get back home depleted following a monotonous day, the last thing you need to do is go through hours in the kitchen planning supper. In the event that you have extra dishes from yesterday, yippee, you simply need to heat them up. In any remaining cases, consider a speedy sheet skillet supper.

The advantages of sheet skillet meals

Sheet skillet supper are quick and simple to plan, which implies they can be a handy solution for non-weekend days when you return home from work and have just 15 minutes to spend preparing food.

Not at all like dishes arranged in a pan, which require adding ingredients in a specific request, intermittent blending, and changes in the temp setting, when the sheet skillet is in the oven, you are free for the following 15 to an hour.

Sheet container meals can be made with not many ingredients, ordinarily stuff that is as of now lying around in your cooler and storeroom.

Making your own supper is a lot more grounded than eating out or requesting takeaway. You will utilize less salt, and less undesirable fats, while adding huge loads of brilliant veggies to your protein.

To wrap things up, sheet skillet suppers require less cleanup than different sorts of dishes. See underneath for accommodating tips on this matter.

Sheet dish fixing gatherings

There are 4 gatherings of ingredients that you need to remember for your sheet dish formula.

1. Above all else is your protein - chicken, meat, pork, salmon, shrimp, tofu, beans or lentils.

2. Next up are your veggies. Broccoli, cauliflower, onions, chimes peppers, mushrooms, squash, Brussels sprouts, beets, carrots, and then some. Essentially anything goes. Albeit boring carbs have become undesirable, potatoes and yams positively have a position of high standing in sheet dish meals.

We love including a head of garlic along with everything else. At the point when prepared, you can spurt out the garlic "spread" onto different veggies.

3. Fat - ideally olive oil or canola oil. Fat is needed for different reasons: It tastes great, it helps the ingredients above heat and cook quicker, and it holds the food back from staying the container!

4. Toppings - these are things that add flavor and punch to your dish. These are items you no doubt have in your kitchen - salt, pepper, flavors, and sauces like teriyaki and others.

Expert tip: you can likewise add garnish to the dish, subsequent to eliminating from the oven. Models are chopped fresh cilantro, chives etc.

1. Pan-Fried Rib-Eye Steak

Prep: 5 mins| Cook: 10 mins| Easy| Serves 2

Ingredients

- 2 rib-eye steaks, each about 200g and 2cm thick
- 1tbsp sunflower oil
- 1 tbsp. /25g margarine
- 1 garlic clove, left entire however slammed once
- Thyme, discretionary

Technique

1. Up to 8 hrs. prior to cooking, wipe the steaks off with kitchen paper and season with salt and pepper. Heat the oil over a high fire in a weighty based skillet that will easily fit the two steaks. At the point when the oil is sparkling, turn the heat down to medium-high and add the spread. When it's sizzling, painstakingly lay the steaks in the pan, wrapping the garlic and spices up along the edges.

2. Remain over the steaks with a couple of utensils, singing and turning them at regular intervals to 1 min so they get a decent brown outside. As a harsh guide, every steak will take 4 mins altogether for uncommon, 5-6 mins altogether for medium and 8-10 mins for all around done. On the off chance that you have an advanced cooking thermometer, the temperatures you're searching for in center of the steak are 50C for uncommon, 60C for medium and 70C for very much done. Leave the steaks to rest for at any rate 5 mins. While the steaks are resting, you can make an exemplary red wine sauce to go with them.

2. Sheet Pan Easter Lamb

Preparation and cooking time| Prep: 20 mins| Cook: 2 hrs. and 15 mins| Plus resting| Easy| Serves 6

Ingredients

- 1.6kg bone-in leg of sheep
- 50ml olive oil, in addition to a sprinkle
- 3 oregano branches, leaves picked and generally chopped
- 4 rosemary branches, leaves of 2 picked and generally chopped
- 1 lemon, zested (save the juice for the spring greens, see works out in a good way for)
- 1 garlic bulb, cloves softly crushed
- 1 red stew, penetrated
- 1kg potatoes, skins on, cut into thick wedges
- 3 fennel bulbs, cut into quarters lengthways, tops eliminated, green fronds saved
- 250ml white wine
- 250ml great quality chicken stock

Technique

1. Remove the sheep from the ice chest 1 hr. prior to cooking it and utilize a sharp blade to make little entry points everywhere on the meat. Blend the oil in with the oregano, chopped rosemary and lemon zing. Rub the marinade everywhere on the sheep, rubbing it well into the cuts.

2. Heat oven to 200C/180C fan/gas 6. Put the garlic, stew, potatoes, fennel and remaining rosemary into a large simmering tin, pour over some olive oil and throw together. Season the sheep liberally, at that point laid it on top of the veg. Cook for 45 mins until the sheep is beginning to brown, at that point pour in the wine and stock. Keep cooking for 30 mins for uncommon (55C on a cooking thermometer), 35-40 mins for medium uncommon (60C) or 45 mins for cooked through (70C).

3. Eliminate the sheep and rest for up to 30 mins. Turn oven down to 160C/140C fan/gas 3, cover the veg with foil and, while the sheep rests, set back in the oven until braised in the cooking juices. Disperse the fennel fronds over the veg, place the sheep back on top and carry the entire tin to the table to serve.

3. Sheet Pan Coriander-Crusted Duck, Roasted Plums & Greens

Prep: 5 mins| Cook: 15 mins| Easy| Serves 2

Ingredients

- 2 tbsp. coriander seeds, softly squashed
- 2 little duck breasts
- 2 plums, stoned, split and cut into wedges
- 2 pak choi , divided lengthways
- 100ml chicken stock
- 2 tbsp. nectar
- 1 tbsp. soy sauce
- 1 tbsp. red wine vinegar
- ¼ tsp. bean stew drops, to serve

Technique

1. Heat the oven to 200C/180C fan/gas 6 and put the coriander seeds on a plate. Score the skin of the duck breasts however many occasions as you can with a little sharp blade, at that point season with salt and press the skin into the coriander seeds. Heat an ovenproof griddle and add the breasts, skin-side down. Put a weighty pan on top to overload them, and cook for 7-8 mins to deliver the fat, sporadically depleting off the abundance.

2. Add the plums and pak choi to the pan flip the breasts over and add a large portion of the stock. Move to the oven and cook for 4-5 mins. Eliminate the duck breasts from the pan and move to a plate to rest alongside the pak choi.

3. Return the pan with the plums to the heat and add the nectar, soy, vinegar and staying stock. Bring to the bubble and keep on cooking until sweet. Cut each duck bosom into four pieces. Mastermind two parts of pak choi over each plate, and settle the lumps of duck bosom and the plums among the greens. Shower with the sauce; at that point sprinkle over the stew drops.

4. Chicken, Morel Mushroom & Asparagus

Prep: 30 mins| Cook: 35 mins| More effort | Serves 5

Ingredients

- 100g new morel or 30g dried morels
- 200ml chicken stock (if using new morels)
- 50g margarine
- 2 shallots finely cut
- 3 thyme branches, leaves picked
- 2 cove leaves
- 1 tbsp. plain flour, in addition to extra for tidying
- 100ml dry sherry or white wine
- 200ml crème fraîche
- 6 skinless boneless chicken thighs cut into large lumps
- Bundle asparagus, woody closures eliminated, stalks cut into 4cm pieces
- ½ pack tarragon, leaves generally chopped, in addition to a branch to brighten
- 1 square puff baked good (375g), all-spread is ideal

- 1 egg, beaten, to coat

Technique

1. On the off chance that you are using dried mushrooms, heat the stock and splash them for 10 mins, at that point eliminate them, strain the fluid and put it away. In case you're using new mushrooms, clean them completely prior to using. Several the most delightful looking morels to the side to finish the highest point of the pie, and split the rest.

2. Heat a large portion of the margarine in a skillet and fry the divided morels for 3-4 mins or until shriveled. Scoop them onto a plate and put away. Heat the leftover spread and delicately cook the shallots in the pan with the thyme and cove. When relaxed, mix in the flour and cook for 1 min or until you have a sandy paste.

3. Pour in the sherry and sizzle, at that point cautiously mix in the stressed dousing fluid (or 200ml chicken stock in the event that you've utilized new morels), trailed by the crème fraîche. Season well and carry the sauce to a delicate stew. Add the chicken and poach in the sauce for 10 mins or until the chicken is simply cooked through. Eliminate the straight, mix through the asparagus, tarragon and singed morels, at that point eliminate from the heat.

4. Heat oven to 220C/200C fan/gas 8. The cake needs to sit on top of the ingredients, so if your pan is excessively profound, utilize a pie dish all things considered. Carry out the cake

on a floured surface to the thickness of a £1 coin, at that point slice the baked good to fit the pan or dish, and wrap it over the pie blend using a moving pin to help you. Generously brush with egg, season the baked good with flaky ocean salt, and pop your saved morels on the top. Prepare for 20 mins or until the baked good has puffed and is a profound brilliant brown. Leave peak rest for 5 mins prior to serving directly from the pan.

5. Formula TIPS
6. SOURCING MORELS
7. Despite the fact that they're in season, new morels must be purchased from expert greengrocers and providers. Nonetheless, the simpler alternative of dried morels works comparably well, with the special reward of giving you a stock from the dousing fluid. The pan you use for this formula is significant: a skillet is ideal – more profound than a griddle yet shallower than a saucepan – and it can go on the hob and in the oven. In the event that you don't have one, make the filling blend in one pan; tip it into an exemplary pie dish prior to fixing with baked good.

5.   Pigeon Breast With Spinach & Bacon

Prep: 5 mins| Cook: 15 mins| Easy| Serves 2

Ingredients

- 50g margarine
- 100g smoked bacon lardoons or chopped smoked bacon
- 2 cuts white sourdough
- 2 pigeon breasts
- 50g chestnut or wild mushrooms, cut
- 200g spinach
- 1 tbsp. red wine or sherry vinegar

Technique

1. Heat a large portion of the spread in a large skillet, at that point fry the bacon for 5 mins until beginning to fresh. Move to a plate using an opened spoon. Fry the bread in any extra bacon fat for 1 min on each side until fresh and brilliant, at that point move to a plate and put away.

2. Season the pigeon liberally with salt and pepper, and heat the excess spread in the pan until sizzling. Burn the pigeon for 2-3 mins on each side until brilliant, at that point move to a slashing load up and leave to rest.

3. Return the seared bacon to the pan and turn up the heat. Dissipate over the mushrooms and fry for 3-4 mins until relaxed, at that point add the spinach, season and sprinkle in the vinegar. Turn the heat up to high and pan fried food until the spinach is withered. Split the spinach combination between the seared bread cuts. Finely cut the pigeon breasts, mastermind over the spinach and serve.

6. The Big Brunch Mushroom Yorkshire Pudding

Prep: 15 mins| Cook: 30 mins| Easy| Serves 2

Ingredients

- 25g spread
- 1 shallot, finely chopped
- 1 garlic clove, finely chopped
- 250g mushrooms, cut (utilize whatever benevolent you can get)
- 1 tbsp. dry sherry or white wine (discretionary)
- Little small bunch of parsley, chopped, in addition to extra to serve
- For the Yorkshire pudding
- 2 eggs
- 100g plain flour
- 150ml milk
- ¼ tsp. powdered porcini (discretionary)
- 1 tbsp. sunflower oil
- For the poached eggs
- Sprinkle of white wine vinegar
- 2 eggs

Strategy

1. To make the Yorkshire pudding, whisk the eggs with the flour until smooth; at that point continuously speed in the milk. Season, at that point add the porcini powder, if using. The hitter can be made as long as a day ahead and chilled.
2. Heat the oven to 220C/200C fan/gas 8, and heat the oil in a 20cm ovenproof griddle or skillet until hot. Pour in the hitter, move to the oven and cook for 20 mins until puffed up and brilliant. Diminish the oven to 180C/160C fan/gas 4, and cook for 5 mins more.
3. In the last 10 mins of the pudding's cooking time, heat the margarine in a subsequent skillet until frothing, at that point pan sear the shallots, garlic and mushrooms for 3-4 mins until the mushrooms are brilliant. Sprinkle in the sherry or wine, if using, and stew briefly. Eliminate from the heat, mix in the parsley and season. Put away.
4. Around 5 mins before the Yorkshire pudding is prepared make the poached eggs. Carry a little pan of water to the overflow with the vinegar. Decrease the heat to a stew, break in the eggs and cook for 2-3 mins until just poached. Eliminate to a plate fixed with kitchen paper using an opened spoon, and channel. Spoon the mushrooms into the Yorkshire pudding, at that point cautiously top with the poached eggs, season, sprinkle with the additional parsley and serve directly from the pan.

7.   Fried Potato Gnocchi

Prep: 30 mins| Cook: 20 mins| Easy| Serves 4 as a side

Ingredients
- 500g Maris Piper potatoes, cut into even-sized pieces
- 1 large egg, beaten
- 125g plain flour, in addition to a lot of extra for molding
- Sprinkle of olive oil
- Handle of spread, for broiling
- Hardly any rosemary leaves, discretionary

Strategy
1. Steam the potatoes for 15-20 mins until delicate. Crush well, in a perfect world with a ricer, which will give fluffier gnocchi. Add the egg and some flavoring blend momentarily with a fork, at that point filter over the flour and unite to make mixture. It should feel dry to the touch yet not brittle. Add more flour if necessary, at that point ply a couple of times on a floured work surface.
2. Carry a large pan of water to the bubble. Split the batter into tennis-ball-sized pieces; at that point fold into finger width ropes. Residue with

a little flour, at that point cut into reduced down pieces. Bubble in clumps for around 1 min or until they weave to the surface. Lift from the pan with an opened spoon and leave to cool in a solitary layer on a large plate or plate. Sprinkle the oil over the cooled gnocchi and throw delicately with your hands to cover.

3. At the point when prepared to serve, heat the spread in a griddle, add the rosemary (on the off chance that using), fry the gnocchi in a couple of groups until fresh and brilliant. Keep warm and serve

8.   Pizza With Aubergine, Ricotta & Mint

Prep: 25 mins| Cook: 35 mins| Plus rising\ Easy|
Serves 2

Ingredients

- For the batter
- 200g solid white bread flour, in addition to a little for tidying
- ½ tsp. quick activity dried yeast
- ¼ tsp. brilliant caster sugar
- A little oil, for lubing
- For the fixings
- 4 tbsp. olive oil, in addition to some extra
- 1 garlic clove, daintily cut
- 200g passata
- Touch of brilliant caster sugar (discretionary)
- 1 little aubergine, cut into plates
- 100g ricotta
- Little small bunch mint, generally chopped

- Additional virgin olive oil, for showering

Strategy

1. Gauge the ingredients for the batter into a large bowl and add 1/2 tsp. salt and 125ml warm water. Blend to frame a delicate mixture, at that point tip onto your work surface and massage for 5 mins or until the batter feels stretchy. Clean and oil the bowl and return the batter. Cover with stick film and leave some place warm to ascend for 1 hr., or until the batter has multiplied in size.

2. In the mean time, make the sauce. Heat 1 tbsp. olive oil in a pan and add the garlic. Sizzle tenderly for 30 secs, ensuring the garlic doesn't brown, at that point add the passata. Season well and air pocket for 8-10 mins until you have a rich sauce – add a touch of sugar on the off chance that it tastes excessively tart. Put away.

3. At the point when the mixture has risen, take out the air and fold it into a pizza base a similar size as a large griddle. Oil the outside of the batter, cover with stick film, at that point leave on the turn out surface for 15 mins to puff up a bit. In the interim, heat 2 tbsp. oil in the skillet and add the aubergines in a solitary layer (you may need to cook in bunches). Season well and cook for 4-5 mins on each side until truly delicate and brilliant. Move to a dish and cover with foil to keep warm.

4. Heat the excess 1 tbsp. of oil in the pan and cautiously lift the mixture into it. You may

need to reshape it a little to fit. Cook over a low-medium heat until the underside is brilliant brown and the edges of the mixture are beginning to look dry and set – this should take around 6 mins, yet it's ideal to pass by eye. Flip over, sprinkle somewhat more oil around the edge of the pan so it streams under the pizza base, and cook for another 5-6 mins until brilliant and cooked through. Reheat the sauce on the off chance that you need to and spread it over the base. Top with the warm aubergines and speck with spoonful's of ricotta. Dissipate with mint and shower with some additional virgin olive oil not long prior to serving.

9. Fried Chicken In Mushroom Sauce

Total time1 hr. and 45 mins | Ready in 1½ - 1¾ hrs.| More effort| Serves 6

Ingredients

- 2 tbsp. sunflower oil
- 6 large, unfenced chicken legs, split at the joint so you have 6 thighs and 6 drumsticks
- 700ml/1¼ pts chicken stock (or water)
- 50g spread
- 1 onion, finely diced
- 400g blended wild mushrooms
- 300ml/½pt.t dry white wine
- 284ml pot twofold cream

Strategy

Heat the oil in a large non-stick skillet. Fry the thighs for 8-10 mins, skin side just, until brilliant brown, at that point move to a goulash dish. Fry the drumsticks for around 5 mins each side and add them to the thighs.

Pour the stock over the chicken legs in the dish. There ought to be sufficient stock to simply cover the chicken, if not add a little water. Carry stock to the bubble and cover, leaving top somewhat unlatched. Cook at just underneath stewing point for 30-35 mins until chicken is cooked.

While chicken is stewing, channel oil from the pan. Heat the margarine in pan and add onion. Sweat onion for 5 mins until delicate, however not shaded. Turn up the heat, add the mushrooms, at that point fry for 3 mins until they relax and begin to smell brilliant. Pour over the white wine, raise the heat to greatest and bubble quickly for 6-8 mins until decreased by 66%. Mood killer the heat and leave until chicken has cooked.

When chicken legs are cooked, strain stock into pan with the onion, mushrooms and white wine, take back to the bubble and diminish again by 66% until it is thick and sweet. Pour in twofold cream; carry it to the bubble, season on the off chance that you need, pour it over chicken. Heat chicken through in the sauce for 2-3 mins at that point turns off the heat and leave for a couple of mins prior to serving. This is a particularly sweet-smelling and delightful looking dish you should serve it directly from the meal with the top on.

10. Next Level Paella

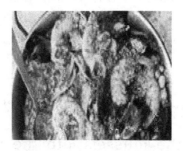

Prep: 40 mins | Cook: 50 mins |More effort | Serves 4

Ingredients

- 3 tbsp. olive oil
- 10 large crude tiger prawns in their shells, heads eliminated and kept
- Little pack of parsley, leaves and stalks isolated, leaves generally chopped
- 100ml dry sherry or white wine
- 500g mussels
- Large touch of saffron strands
- 150g cooking chorizo, cut into pieces
- 1 onion, finely chopped
- 3 garlic cloves, finely chopped
- 1 medium squid (about 300g), cleaned and cut into rings with limbs unblemished
- 2 ready tomatoes, generally chopped
- 250g paella rice
- 100g frozen podded wide beans or peas (or a combination of the two), thawed out
- 1 lemon, finely zested then cut into wedges
- Smoked ocean salt (discretionary)

Strategy

1. Heat 1 tbsp. of the oil in a wide, shallow pan. Add the prawn heads and parsley stalks and sizzle until the heads become pink, at that point crush with a potato masher. Pour over the sherry or wine and 300ml water, season with salt and stew for 10 mins to make a stock, squashing the prawn heads as they cook.

2. Disperse the mussels into the pan; cover the pan freely with a top or tea towel, at that point put over a high heat for 3-4 mins until the mussels simply open. Mix to deliver the mussel juices, at that point pour the substance of the pan into a colander set over a large bowl containing the saffron. Allow the saffron to soak in the stock – you will require 700ml altogether, so top up with water if necessary and give everything a decent mix. Choose the mussels from the colander, at that point put away.

3. Crash the pan and add the remainder of the olive oil. Sizzle the chorizo until it delivers its oil, at that point add the onion and garlic and cook until relaxed. Add the squid and turn over until it becomes white. Add the tomatoes and cook down briefly, at that point pour over the greater part of the stock, give everything a decent mix and bring to the bubble. Dissipate the rice over the stock, mix well once, at that point bubble overwhelmingly for 5 mins. Diminish the heat to the least setting and gradually stew for 10 mins without blending

until the rice has ingested a large portion of the fluid.

4. Fold the prawn tails into the rice and stew for 5 mins, turning them over until cooked through. Mix through the mussels and expansive beans or peas. Taste the rice – on the off chance that it is still a little crude however the pan is dry, add a sprinkle more stock and keep on cooking; assuming it's excessively soupy, increment the heat to cook off the remainder of the stock.

5. When the rice is simply cooked, turn off the heat and cover with a tea towel for a couple of moments. Disperse over the parsley leaves and lemon zing, at that point season with smoked salt on the off chance that you like. Mix everything once; at that point serve directly from the pan, with lemon wedges as an afterthought.

11. Salmon, Samphire & Charred Cucumber Salad

Prep: 30 min |Cook: 30 mins| Plus 1 hr. chilling|
More effort| Serves 6

Ingredients

- 1 tbsp. ocean growth drops or nori sushi sheets, squashed
- 2 tsp. bean stew drops
- 1 tbsp. demerara sugar
- Finely ground zings 2 limes
- 750g boneless side of salmon
- 1 tbsp. olive oil
- 2 large cucumbers split lengthways
- 2 green chilies cut
- 3 tbsp. sushi ginger, chopped
- 150g samphire
- 1 tbsp. sesame oil
- 2 lots of peppery leaves, similar to watercress or mizuna

Technique

1. Tip the ocean growth drops, bean stew, sugar, lime zing and 1 tsp. ocean salt into a bowl and combine as one. Lay the salmon substance side up on a plate fixed with foil and disperse over the kelp preparing. Cover the plate with stick film and chill for 1 hr.

2. Heat the oven to 180C/160C fan/gas 6. Sprinkle the salmon with a little olive oil and meal in the oven for 25-30 mins or until just cooked. Eliminate from the oven and leave to cool at room temperature.

3. While the salmon is cooling, heat a weighty skillet or frying pan. Brush the cut side of the cucumber with a little oil, place cut-side down in the pan and singe for 2 mins or until scorched. Try not to stress on the off chance that it darkens – the flavor will be incredible. At the point when the cucumber is prepared, eliminate from the heat and season with somewhat salt. Cut into thick wedges and tip into a large plate of mixed greens bowl. Add the stew, chopped ginger, and samphire and sesame oil and throw everything together

4. Drop the salmon into large scaled down pieces and add to the plate of mixed greens bowl alongside the leaves. Tenderly prepare the serving of mixed greens, being mindful so as not to separate the salmon to an extreme, at that point tip out onto a large platter.

12. Chicken & Broccoli Pasta Bake

Prep: 5 mins| Cook: 35 mins\ Easy| Serves 4

Ingredients

- 350g pasta shells or plumes
- 200g broccoli, cut into exceptionally little florets and the stems daintily cut
- 2 tbsp. olive oil
- 350g boneless, skinless chicken breasts daintily cut
- 175g chestnut mushrooms, quartered
- 4 tbsp. sundried tomato paste
- 80g delicate cheddar with garlic and spices (like Boursin)
- 284ml container single cream
- For the fixing
- Bundle of spring onions, finely cut
- 85g develop cheddar, ground
- 1 garlic clove, finely chopped
- 50g chipped almonds

Technique

1. Heat the oven to 190C/fan170C/gas 5. Bring a large pan of salted water to the bubble. Toss in 350g pasta shells or plumes, mix well and get back to the bubble.
2. Cook for 6 minutes, at that point add 200g broccoli, cut into tiny florets and stems meagerly cut, and cook for 5-6 minutes more until the pasta is simply cooked. Channel well, at that point get back to the pan.
3. Heat 2 tbsp. olive oil in a wide pan, add 350g meagerly cut boneless, skinless chicken breasts and fry until delicately browned.
4. Tip in 175g quartered chestnut mushrooms and sautéed food for 1 moment, at that point mix in 4 tbsp. sundried tomato paste, 80g delicate cheddar with garlic and spices and a 284ml container single cream.
5. Delicately stew, mixing, until the cheddar has liquefied to thicken the sauce. Season with salt and pepper.
6. Pour the sauce over the pasta, blending delicately until covered, at that point tip into a shallow ovenproof dish (about 1.7 liter limits) and level the top.
7. Blend a lot of finely cut spring onions, 85g ground develop cheddar, 1 finely chopped garlic clove and 50g chipped almonds for the fixing and sprinkle over the pasta. Heat for 20 minutes until brilliant.
8. Formula TIPS
9. MAKING IT DIFFERENT
10. Rather than chicken and broccoli, take a stab at using cubed ham and green beans.

11. Works out positively for
12. Lemon curd pots

13. Venison With Rhubarb Chutney

Prep: 45 mins | Cook: 1 hr. and 20 mins\ More effort| Serves 4 (with chutney leftover)

Ingredients

- For the chutney
- 1kg rhubarb, chopped
- 1 red onion, cut
- 225g dull brown delicate sugar
- 2 garlic cloves, squashed
- 300ml red wine vinegar
- 1 pear, stripped, cored and chopped
- 1 apple, stripped, cored and chopped
- 2 tsp. salt
- 50g sultanas
- 1 tsp. juniper berries, squashed
- 2 pieces stem ginger from a container, depleted and chopped, in addition to 1 tbsp. syrup
- For the venison
- 500g midsection filet or venison steaks
- 1 tbsp. olive oil
- 150ml red wine
- 25g spread
- Squashed potato, to serve
- Rocket leaf, to serve

Strategy

1. Put every one of the ingredients for the chutney in a large hefty based saucepan and bring to the bubble, mixing as often as possible. Bubble tenderly for 1 hr. until thick and lustrous, at that point spoon into sanitized containers (see tip) while still hot.

2. Brush the venison filet or steaks with the olive oil and season well. Heat a large skillet over a high heat and fry however you would prefer, at that point lay on a plate, covered with foil. Empty the red wine into a similar pan and bubble quickly to lessen by over half. Rush in the margarine, season to taste, and eliminate from the heat.

3. Cut the venison, put on a serving platter or board and shower over the red wine sauce. Present with the rhubarb chutney, pureed potatoes and some rocket leaves as an afterthought.

4. Formula TIPS

5. TO Sterilize YOU'RE JARS

6. Heat oven to 140C/120C fan/gas 1. Wash the containers in hot, sudsy water and flush well. Put on a preparing sheet and fly in the oven to dry totally. In the case of using Kilner containers, heat up the elastic seals, as dry heat harms them.

7. Go through YOUR CHUTNEY

8. This formula makes enough to fill around 2 x 500ml containers. Serve the extras with hard cheddar and cold meats or close by your Sunday cook sheep or pork.

9. A LITTLE EXTRA

10. To benefit as much as possible from the wonderfully pink rhubarb stems, you could dish or pan-fry some extra chopped rhubarb not long prior to serving, and overlap it through the chutney.

14. Pork & Chorizo Enchiladas

Prep: 30 mins| Cook: 1 hr. and 10 mins | Easy|
Serves 8

Ingredients

- 1 tbsp. olive oil
- 2 large onions, divided and meagerly cut
- 3 garlic cloves, chopped
- 1 tbsp. ground cumin
- 2 piled tbsp. smoked paprika
- 2 tsp. cinnamon
- 2 red chilies, split, deseeded and cut
- 500g pack pork mince
- 2 x 200g packs cooking chorizo wieners, taken out from their skins
- 680g jug passata
- 1 pork or chicken stock shape
- 2 red and 2 green peppers, deseeded, quartered and cut
- 2 x 400g jars borlotti beans, depleted
- 30g pack coriander, chopped
- 500g tub fromage frais (not sans fat)
- 1 large egg
- 2 packs of 8 delicate corn tortillas
- 140g develop cheddar, ground

- Green serving of mixed greens, to serve

Technique

1. Heat the oil in a large, profound pan and fry the onions and garlic for around 10 mins. Add the flavors and a large portion of the stew, and cook for 1 min more. Tip in the pork and chorizo, turn up the heat and fry the meat, blending and separating it until it changes tone. Pour in the passata and 300ml water; at that point disintegrate in the stock solid shape. Heap in the peppers, mix, cover and stew over a low heat for 30 mins until the meat and peppers are delicate. Mix in the beans and 66% of the coriander.

2. In the mean time, tip the fromage frais (with any fluid in the tub) into a bowl, and beat in the egg, remaining coriander and preparing. Get out 2 ovenproof and cooler evidence dishes.

3. Spoon the meat onto the focal point of the tortillas, move up and orchestrate 8 in each dish. Spoon half of the fromage frais blend on top and smooth it to cover the tortillas. Disperse each with a large portion of the cheddar and remaining chilies. In the case of eating currently, heat oven to 190C/170C fan/gas 5 and prepare for 25 mins until brilliant, at that point serve. On the off chance that freezing, when cold cover with stick film and foil. Will save for a very long time. To serve, defrost in the cooler and reheat uncovered as above, adding an additional 15 mins to the time, watching that it is hot

completely through. You can likewise prepare from frozen. Put the dish (covered with new foil) on a preparing plate in the oven, at that point heat oven to 180C/160C fan/gas 4 and prepare for 2 hrs. Try not to place the frozen dish in a preheated oven as it would break – it's smarter to allow it to heat slowly. Eliminate the thwart and heat for 20 mins more. Present with a green plate of mixed greens.

15. Triple Cheese & Aubergine Lasagna

Prep: 45 mins | Cook: 2 hrs. | More effort | Serves 8

Ingredients

- 12-16 new lasagna sheets
- For the tomato and aubergine sauce
- 4 tbsp. olive oil
- 3 large aubergines cut into little lumps
- 2 large onions, chopped
- 4 garlic cloves, finely chopped
- 2 x 400g jars chopped tomatoes
- 2 tbsp. tomato purée
- 1 tsp. brilliant caster sugar
- Touch of stew chips
- Little small bunch basil leaves, finely chopped
- Run of soy sauce
- For the ricotta filling
- 500g ricotta
- 50g parmesan (or veggie lover elective) finely ground
- 2 medium eggs, beaten
- ¼ tsp. ground nutmeg
- For the cheddar sauce

- 500g milk
- 50g plain flour
- 50g margarine
- 100g develop cheddar, ground
- 1 tsp. English mustard

Strategy

1. In the first place, make the tomato and aubergine sauce. Heat 1 tbsp. of the oil in a large non-stick skillet and cook the aubergine in 3 clumps, adding 1 tbsp. oil for each cluster. They ought to be softened and daintily brilliant.

2. Add the excess oil to the pan and cook the onions for 5 mins until softened. Mix in the garlic, cook for 1 min more, at that point return the aubergine to the pan with the tomatoes, tomato purée, and sugar and stew chips. Bring just to the bubble, at that point go down to a stew and cook for 10 mins. Remove the heat, mix in the basil and soy sauce, and season to taste.

3. Combine as one every one of the ingredients for the ricotta filling, season and put away – or cover and leave in the ice chest if making ahead of time. Both the aubergine and the ricotta sauce can be chilled for as long as 2 days.

4. For the cheddar sauce, add every one of the ingredients to a pan and cook over a medium heat, blending constantly, until it thickens and the cheddar has liquefied, at that point turn down the heat to low and cook for another 5 mins. Season to taste.

5. Heat oven to 180C/160C fan/gas 4. To collect the lasagne, spoon a large portion of the aubergine blend into the lower part of a large heating dish. Top with a layer of lasagne sheets, at that point spread over a ricotta layer. Add another layer of lasagne sheets, trailed by the excess aubergine blend and another layer of lasagne sheets. Pour over the cheddar sauce (it would now be able to be frozen for multi month – thaw out prior to cooking). Prepare in the oven for 50 mins-1 hr. until brilliant and heated through.

16. Pan-Fried Mackerel Fillets With Beetroot & Fennel

Prep: 10 mins| Cook: 3 mins | Easy |Serves 2

Ingredients

- 2 mackerel filets (about 300g/11oz)
- 2 tsp. cold-squeezed rapeseed oil
- 1/2 little fennel bulb, quartered and daintily cut
- 1 little beetroot, stripped and meagerly cut
- 100g cucumber, split and meagerly cut
- 1 eating apple, cored, quartered and cut
- 1 tbsp. lemon juice in addition to lemon wedges, to serve
- 100g full-fat normal bio yogurt
- Little pack dill

Technique

1. Put one of the mackerel filets on a board and cut a 'V' down the middle, either side of the pin bones, to make two more modest filets, at that point eliminate the bones. Rehash with the other filet. Rub with the oil and season with a lot of ground dark pepper. Put away.

2. Put the fennel in a bowl with the beetroot, cucumber and apple. Sprinkle over the lemon juice, add the yogurt and blend well. Generally hack the dill, setting to the side a couple of fronds to trimming, and disperse over the serving of mixed greens, at that point season with ground dark pepper and throw together delicately. Put away.
3. Put a large non-stick griddle over a medium-high heat. When hot, add the fish, skin-side down, and cook for 2 1/2 mins. Flip the fish over and cook for 30 secs on the opposite side.
4. Put the filets on top of the plate of mixed greens and present with the dill fronds and lemon wedges for pressing over.

17. Chicken & Ham Lasagna

Prep: 20 mins | Cook: 50 mins | Easy | Serves 6 – 8

Ingredients

- 6 boneless skinless chicken breasts (around 700g)
- ½ medium onion, cut
- 2 narrows leaves
- 200ml white wine
- 100g margarine
- 100g plain flour
- 500ml semi-skimmed milk
- 140g cut smoked ham, cut into strips
- 200g youthful spinach leaves
- 225g no pre-cook dried lasagne sheets (around 20 sheets)
- 200g prepared ground mozzarella
- 25g parmesan, finely ground

Technique

1. Put the chicken breasts in a medium saucepan with the onion, narrows leaves and wine. Pour over barely enough water to cover, around 200ml. put a top on top and bring to a delicate stew. Poach delicately for 15 mins or until the chicken is simply cooked. Move the chicken to a board and strain the fluid into a container.

2. Soften the margarine in a large non-stick saucepan over a medium heat. Mix in the flour with a wooden spoon and cook for about a moment. Slowly add the milk, a little at an at once, between every option to guarantee the sauce stays smooth. When all the milk has been added, mix in the held cooking fluid and keep cooking for a further 2-3 mins. Change the flavoring to taste. Heat oven to 200C/180C fan/gas 6.

3. Cut the chicken into little lumps and mix into the saucepan. Add the ham and spinach and cook until the spinach has withered. Spoon 33% of the chicken combination into the foundation of a 3-liter lasagne dish (around 26 x 18cm). Top with 33% of the lasagne sheets. Rehash the layers twice more, finishing with lasagne. Disperse the mozzarella and Parmesan on top and season with dark pepper. Can be frozen at this stage (see beneath). Prepare for around 25 mins or until the lasagne is delicate, the fixing is very much browned and the filling hot.

4. Formula TIPS

5. TO FREEZE

6. Follow the means up to when the lasagne is heated, at that point leave to cool and cover with a twofold layer of foil. Freeze for as long as 2 months. To serve, open up the frozen lasagne and cover with stick film. Defrost in the ice chest short-term. Eliminate the stick film, cover with thwart and heat as above for 40 mins. Eliminate the thwart and heat for another 10 mins.

18. Black Bean & Barley Cakes With Poached Eggs

Prep: 10 mins | Cook: 10 mins | Easy | Serves 4

Ingredients

- 2 x 400g jars dark beans, depleted well
- 15g porridge oats
- 2 tsp. ground coriander
- 1 tsp. cumin seeds
- 2 tsp. thyme leaves
- 1 tsp. vegetable bouillon powder
- 5 large eggs
- 2 spring onions, the white part finely chopped, the green meagerly cut
- 400g can grain, depleted
- 2-3 tsp. rapeseed oil
- 200g pack cherry tomatoes on the plant
- 4 tbsp. sunflower seeds

Technique

1. Tip the beans, oats, ground coriander, cumin seeds, thyme and vegetable bouillon powder into a bowl and barrage along with a hand blender to make a harsh paste. Mix in 1 egg with the whites of the spring onion and grain. In case you're following our Healthy Diet Plan, separate a large portion of the blend for another morning and chill.

2. Heat a large portion of the oil in your largest griddle and fry the other portion of the combination in two major spoonfuls's, delicately squeezed to make level cakes. After 7 mins, cautiously go over to cook the opposite side for 4-5 mins.

3. Then, poach two eggs in a pan of bubbling water for 3-4 mins, and tenderly fry half of the tomatoes on the plant in a little oil for a couple of mins to brown somewhat. Slide the cakes onto plates and top with the tomatoes, eggs, a dissipating of the spring onion greens and a large portion of the sun owner seeds. On another morning, rehash stages 2 and 3 with the leftover ingredients.

4. In case you're not after the Healthy Diet Plan and you're serving four, follow stages 2 and 3 with every one of the ingredients rather than just half.

19. Jerk Roast Chicken

Prep: 30 mins | Cook: 2 hrs. and 10 mins | Plus at least 2 hrs. marinating | Easy | Serves 4 – 6

Ingredients

- 1 ½kg entire chicken
- 2 red onions, split, at that point cut into wedges, leaving the root unblemished
- 2 red peppers, deseeded and chopped into pieces
- 4 yams, stripped and cut into pieces
- 400g can dark beans, depleted and washed
- 400ml coconut milk
- Cooked rice, to serve
- Flatbreads, to serve
- For the jerk paste
- 1 red onion, chopped into large pieces
- 5 garlic cloves, stripped
- 1 scotch cap stew, deseeded
- 3 fat green chilies, deseeded
- Pack coriander, follows generally chopped, and leaves held, to serve
- Large pack thyme leaves picked
- Zing and juice 2 limes (save the squeezed parts for the chicken)

- 1 tbsp. nectar
- 2 tbsp. olive or rapeseed oil, in addition to a shower
- ½ nutmeg, ground
- 1 tsp. ground allspice

Strategy

1. First make the jerk paste. Put every one of the ingredients in a food processor, add a decent touch of salt and mix to a fine purée, adding a sprinkle of water if the combination is battling to separate. Tie the legs together in the event that you like, and put in a large flameproof broiling tin. Pour over the jerk paste and rub all finished and inside the chicken. Stuff the cavity with the squeezed lime parts and cover the plate with foil. Chill for up to 48 hrs. or at least 2 hrs.

2. Heat oven to 200C/180C fan/gas 6. Cook the chicken for 45 mins.

3. Take the chicken out the oven, eliminate the foil and cautiously lift it onto a plate, pouring any juice from the hole into the tin. Tip the onions, peppers and yams into the tin, and season well, at that point throw in the plate to cover in any lingering jerk paste. Put the chicken on top of the veggies and sprinkle it with a little oil. Lower the oven to 180C/160C fan/gas 4 and return the simmering tin to the center rack, revealed. Broil for a further 45 mins or until the vegetables are delicate and the chicken is cooked through – on the off chance that you have a meat thermometer, watch that the temperature has arrived at 75C.

Cautiously eliminate the chicken from the tin, place on a plate and enclose by foil, at that point leave to rest.

4. Spot the simmering tin on the hob over a medium heat. Mix in the beans and coconut milk, scratching the lower part of the tin to take off any delectable pieces. Stew until the sauce has thickened a little, at that point season to taste. In the event that the sauce looks sleek, skim the fat off the surface with a spoon. Set the chicken back in the pan and disperse over the coriander leaves prior to taking to the table. Present with rice and flatbreads for cleaning up the sauce.

20. Frying Pan Pizza Pie

Prep: 1 hr. and 10 mins | Cook: 20 mins | Plus 1 hr. rising | Easy | Serves 4

Ingredients

- 290g pack pizza mixture blend
- Flour, for tidying
- 1 tbsp. pesto or tapenade
- 125g ball mozzarella daintily cut
- 4-6 sundried tomatoes, generally chopped

Technique

1. Make up the pizza blend adhering to pack guidelines. Put in a bowl, cover with a perfect tea towel or stick film and leave some place warm to ascend for 1 hr., or until multiplied in size. Gap fifty-fifty and roll or press out each piece on a daintily floured surface to a 20-23cm round (contingent upon the size of your griddle). Spread one round with pesto or tapenade to inside 2cm of the edges, at that point top with mozzarella and tomatoes. Cover with the other piece of batter and press the edges to seal in the filling.
2. Heat the griddle, put in the pizza pie and cook on a genuinely low heat for 10 mins. Rearrange onto a large plate, at that point

slide once more into the pan and cook for 10 mins more until very much browned. Leave to cool for 10 mins, at that point slice into wedges to serve.

3. Formula TIPS
4. Moving TIPS
5. On the off chance that you don't have a moving pin, utilize a wine bottle or essentially press out the batter using your fingers. On the off chance that you like, you can cook this pizza pie on a grill – which adds a superb chargrilled flavor – simply ensure your coals are not very hot.
6. MAKE IT YOUR OWN
7. Add anything you would typically put on a pizza, like chorizo, salami, prosciutto, ground hard cheddar, for example, cheddar or Gruyère rather than the mozzarella, or wholegrain mustard rather than the pesto however take care not to over-burden it or the rounding may spill out.
8. Works out in a good way for
9. Shop couscous
10. Tomato and onion salad

21. Sheet Pan-Cooked Mackerel with Beetroot Salsa & Bean Mash

Prep: 10 mins | Cook: 7 mins | Easy | Serves 2

Ingredients

- 2 large mackerel filets (to set aside cash, purchase an entire fish and request that the fishmonger set it up for you)
- 65g pack rocket
- For the salsa and beans
- 250g cooked beetroot, diced
- ½ red onion, finely chopped
- Ground zing and juice 0.5 lime
- 2 tbsp. chopped dill, in addition to extra for sprinkling
- 1 tsp. olive oil, in addition to some extra for cooking
- 1 garlic clove, finely chopped
- 400g can cannellini beans

Strategy

1. Blend the beetroot and the onion in a bowl with the lime zing, a decent press of juice, preparing and dill.

2. Heat the tsp. oil in a non-stick pan and tenderly cook the garlic until softened, at that point tip in the beans, and a portion of the juice from the can with preparing. Squash the beans keeping them very stout, at that point keep warm.

3. Feel along the fish to check for bones, and in the event that you discover any, solidly haul them out with your fingers or tweezers. Heat a non-stick griddle, wipe with a little oil at that point cook the mackerel skin-side down for 3-4 mins. Flip over and cook for a couple of moments more until the filets are cooked entirely through. Spoon the bean squash onto plates, top with the fish and a large portion of the salsa at that point disperse with additional dill. Present with the rocket as an afterthought and the remainder of the salsa in a bowl.

22. Pan-Fried Scallops With Parsnip Purée & Pancetta Crumbs

Prep: 10 mins | Cook: 30 mins | More effort| Serves 3

Ingredients

- 1 tbsp. vegetable oil
- 9 large scallops, coral eliminated (see tip, beneath)
- Juice ½ lemons
- For the pancetta morsels
- 50g pancetta cut into 5cm cuts
- 50g new breadcrumb
- 1 tbsp. thyme leaf, chopped
- For the parsnip purèe
- 200g parsnip, cut into lumps
- 200ml full-fat milk
- Little handle of margarine

Technique

1. To make the pancetta pieces (which you can do as long as a day ahead), set a large skillet over a medium heat. Add the pancetta and sizzle for 5 mins, turning, until hued. Sprinkle the breadcrumbs into the pan and keep singing and mixing until browned and fresh. Rush the combination in a food processor to fine morsels. Blend in the thyme and store in an impermeable holder if making ahead.

2. To make the parsnip purée, tip the parsnips into a little saucepan with the milk and some flavoring. Bring to the bubble, lessen heat and stew for 10-15 mins until the parsnips are delicate. Purée the combination in the food processor, at that point add the margarine. Rub through a fine strainer into a perfect saucepan, prepared to reheat.

3. Heat the oil in a large griddle over a high heat. Season the scallops and lay those in a circle around the edge of the pan (see stage 1). At the point when the last scallop has been added, leave for 1 min until browned. At that point, beginning with the principal scallop, delicately turn (stage 2). At the point when every one of the scallops are cooked, move to a warm plate and rapidly add the lemon juice to your hot pan, scratching the base to shape a sauce and adding a sprinkle of water if necessary.

4. Reheat the parsnip purée, at that point swipe onto 3 plates (stage 3). Top with the scallops, pancetta morsels and juices from the pan. Serve straight away.

5. Formula TIPS
6. Planning SCALLOPS
7. Scallops can accompany their dazzling orange coral joined – these are totally eatable and don't should be cooked any in an unexpected way. Not every person prefers the coral, in any case, so on the off chance that you don't need it, basically cut it from the scallop with a sharp blade or scissors.

23. Whole baked ricotta with lentils & roasted cherry tomatoes

Prep: 15 mins | Cook: 50 mins | Easy | Serves 4

Ingredients

- 6 banana shallots, quartered
- 90ml olive oil, in addition to extra for showering
- 1 large lemon, zested and squeezed
- Little pack basil, generally chopped
- Little pack dill, generally chopped
- 2 x 250g pockets cooked puy lentils
- 150g spinach
- 2 x 250g entire ricotta
- 400g cherry tomatoes on the plant

Strategy

1. Heat oven to 200C/180C fan/gas 6. Put the shallots in a medium-sized broiling tin, sprinkle more than 2 tbsp. olive oil and season. Broil for 15 mins until brilliant brown and starting to mellow. In the mean time, to make a dressing, whisk the excess olive oil with the lemon zing and juice, mix through a large portion of the spices and season.
2. Throw the lentils along with the shallots, spinach and 4 tbsp. water. Put the ricotta in the focal point of the cooking tin and lay the tomatoes around them. Shower the dressing over the lentils and shake the tin a little to consolidate everything. Shower a little olive oil over the ricotta and season everything great. Get back to the oven for 30-35 mins or until the ricotta is firm and daintily brilliant.
3. Serve the lentils in shallow dishes finished off with spoonful's of the velvety ricotta and sprinkled with the leftover spices.
4. Works out positively for
5. Rural bread
6. Green plate of mixed greens with olive dressing
7. Ricotta and basil pizza bread

24. Confit Chicken Legs With Potato Hash & Poached Egg

Prep: 15 mins | Cook: 3 hrs. | Plus 1 hr. brining |
More effort | Serves 2

Ingredients

- For the comfit
- 4 thyme branches, in addition to 1 tbsp. picked thyme leaves
- 25g ocean salt
- Zing 1 lemon
- 2 chicken legs
- 1 shallot
- 1 garlic bulb, split fifty-fifty
- 1 tarragon branch
- 600ml olive oil
- For the potato hash
- 400g potatoes, diced
- 50g dirty bacon, cut into lardoons
- 1 leek, cleaned and cut
- 1 green bean stew, chopped
- 50g spinach
- 25g kale, shredded
- ½ little level leaf parsley, a modest bunch held to serve

- ½ tbsp. sherry or vermouth vinegar
- 2 eggs

Technique

1. Blend the thyme leaves with the salt and lemon zing. Rub over the chicken legs, at that point chill for 1 hr. Heat oven to 140C/120C fan/gas 1.

2. Wipe the chicken off with kitchen paper. Spot in a little cooking tin with the excess comfit ingredients. Prepare in the oven for 2-2 1/2 hrs. until delicate, at that point eliminate from the oil and channel on a wire rack. Save and strain the oil – this is extraordinary for simmering veg or making more confit. Save the shallot and garlic.

3. To make the hash, heat 1 tbsp. of the injected oil in a hefty lined griddle. Add the potatoes and cook for around 10 mins until they begin to mellow. Add the bacon and cook, mixing, until it's crisping. Add the leeks, stew, confit shallot and garlic (extracted from its skin). Cook for another 5 mins until the leeks have softened and the potatoes are cooked through. Season; at that point add the spinach, kale and parsley. Mix until the leaves have shriveled. Add a sprinkle of vinegar.

4. Poach the eggs in scarcely stewing water for 3 mins, at that point channel on kitchen paper. Serve the chicken with the hash, eggs and a sprinkling of parsley.

25. One-Pan Coriander-Crusted Duck, Roasted Plums & Greens

Prep: 5 mins| Cook: 15 mins | Easy | Serves 2

Ingredients

- 2 tbsp. coriander seeds, gently squashed
- 2 little duck breasts
- 2 plums, stoned, split and cut into wedges
- 2 pak choi, divided lengthways
- 100ml chicken stock
- 2 tbsp. nectar
- 1 tbsp. soy sauce
- 1 tbsp. red wine vinegar
- ¼ tsp. bean stew pieces, to serve

Technique

1. Heat the oven to 200C/180C fan/gas 6 and put the coriander seeds on a plate. Score the skin of the duck breasts however many occasions as you can with a little sharp blade, at that point season with salt and press the skin into the coriander seeds. Heat an ovenproof skillet and add the breasts, skin-side down. Put a hefty pan on top to overload them, and cook for 7-8 mins to deliver the fat, every so often depleting off the overabundance.

2. Add the plums and pak choi to the pan flip the breasts over and add a large portion of the stock. Move to the oven and cook for 4-5 mins. Eliminate the duck breasts from the pan and move to a plate to rest alongside the pak choi.

3. Return the pan with the plums to the heat and add the nectar, soy, vinegar and staying stock. Bring to the bubble and keep on cooking until sweet. Cut each duck bosom into four pieces. Orchestrate two parts of pak choi over each plate, and settle the pieces of duck bosom and the plums among the greens. Shower with the sauce; at that point sprinkle over the bean stew pieces.

26. Sheet Pan Spaghetti With Nduja, Fennel & Olives

Prep: 15 mins | Cook: 15 mins | Easy | Serves 4

Ingredients

- 400g spaghetti
- 3 garlic cloves meagerly cut
- ½ fennel, divided and meagerly cut
- 75g nduja or sobrasada paste
- 200g tomatoes (all that you can get), chopped into lumps
- 75g dark olives, hollowed and cut
- 2 tsp. tomato purée
- 3 tbsp. olive oil, in addition to a sprinkle
- 2 tsp. red wine vinegar
- 40g pecorino, in addition to extra to serve
- modest bunch basil, torn

Technique

1. Heat up the pot. Put every one of the ingredients aside from the pecorino and basil in a wide saucepan or profound griddle and season well. Pour over 800ml pot high temp water and bring to a stew, using your utensils

to facilitate the spaghetti under the fluid as it begins to relax.

2. Stew, revealed, for 10-12 mins, throwing the spaghetti through the fluid now and then until it is cooked and the sauce is diminished and sticking to it. Add a sprinkle more high temp water if the sauce is excessively thick or doesn't cover the pasta while it cooks. Turn up the heat for the last couple of mins to drive off the abundance fluid, leaving you with a rich sauce. Mix through the pecorino and basil, and present with an additional shower of oil and pecorino as an afterthought.
3. Formula TIPS
4. NDUJA PASTE
5. Nduja, a zesty spreadable salami paste from Calabria, in Italy, is accessible at ocado.com and from stores. Sobrasada, which is the spanish same, has the kind of chorizo. Discover it in chose Sainsbury's or stores. Or on the other hand you can utilize finely chopped chorizo all things being equal.

Conclusion

I would like to thank you for going through all the recipes. Hope you liked all sheet pan recipes. These are easy to prepare and can easily be made at home. These tastes incredible so try at home and appreciate.

I wish you all good luck

CPSIA information can be obtained
at www.ICGtesting.com
Printed in the USA
BVHW090305050621
608821BV00011B/2459

9 781802 005264